SCOOBY-DOO!

FOOD Jokes!

by Michael Dahl

illustrated by Scott Jeralds

Raintree is an imprint of Capstone Global Library Limited, a company incorporated in England and Wales having its registered office at 7 Pilgrim Street, London, EC4V 6LB – Registered company number: 6695582

www.raintree.co.uk
myorders@raintree.co.uk

Edited by James Benefield and Eliza Leahy
Designed by Bob Lentz
Original illustrations © Hanna-Barbera 2015
Illustrated by Scott Jeralds
Production by Gene Bentdahl
Printed in China by Nordica
0914/CA21401580

ISBN 978-1-4062-9240-4 (paperback)
18 17 16 15 14
10 9 8 7 6 5 4 3 2 1

British Library Cataloguing in Publication Data
A full catalogue record for this book is available from the British Library.

Acknowledgements
Every effort has been made to contact copyright holders of material reproduced in this book. Any omissions will be rectified in subsequent printings if notice is given to the publisher.

All the Internet addresses (URLs) given in this book were valid at the time of going to press. However, due to the dynamic nature of the Internet, some addresses may have changed, or sites may have changed or ceased to exist since publication. While the author and publisher regret any inconvenience this may cause readers, no responsibility for any such changes can be accepted by either the author or the publisher.

Set List:

What did the nut say when she sneezed?
"Cashew!"

What did the spaghetti say when it got tangled up?
"Knot again!"

What did the tomato say to the bacon?
"Lettuce get together soon!"

What did one steak knife say to the other?
"You look sharp!"

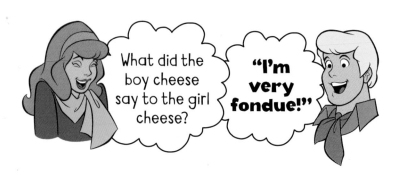

What did one plate say
to the other plate?
"Dinner's on me!"

What did the orange peel say
to the orange?
"I gotcha covered!"

What did the cheese wheel say when he crossed
the finish line?
"I'm so Gouda at this!"

What did the mother tomato say to the baby tomato
behind her?

"Come on, ketchup!"

CUSTOMER: Excuse me, waiter, but will my pizza be long?
WAITER: No, sir, it will be round.

Have you heard about the neutron that went to the
restaurant and ordered a pizza?

"How much do I owe you?" asked the neutron.

The waiter said, **"For you? No charge."**

Why don't you ever see a snail queuing up at a drive-
through restaurant?
Because they don't like *fast* food!

What did the richest man in the world make for
dinner every night?
Table reservations.

Why was the restaurant chef arrested?

Because he was beating the eggs and whipping the cream!

Why was the customer so angry with the Italian restaurant?

I don't know, but she certainly gave the waiter a pizza her mind!

CUSTOMER: Sir, why is my food so messy?

WAITER: You told me to *step on it*!

What did the zombie order for lunch?

Pizza, with everyone on it!

Bit three:
Nutritious knee-slappers

Why did Scooby smear raspberries all over the road?
To go with the traffic jam!

How do you know that carrots are good for your eyes?
Well, have you ever seen a rabbit wearing glasses?

How do you unlock a banana?
With a mon-key!

What does a confused hen lay?
Scrambled eggs!

What kind of nuts do you eat in outer space?
Astronuts.

Why did the orange stop in the middle of the road?

It ran out of juice.

Why did Little Miss Muffet push Humpty Dumpty
off the wall?
He got in her whey.

What happens when a banana gets sunburned?

It peels!

If I had five apples in one hand and six oranges in the other, what would I have?

Really big hands!

What do you call the best pupil at corn school?
The "A" corn!

Why did the woman divorce the grape?
She was tired of raisin' kids!

Why did the tomato turn red?
It saw the salad dressing!

How do you make an artichoke?
Grab it by the throat!

What's red, round and has a sore throat?
A hoarse radish!

Why were the raspberries so sad?
Because their mum was in a jam!

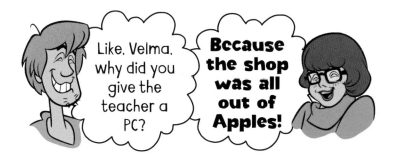

Like, Velma, why did you give the teacher a PC?

Because the shop was all out of Apples!

Shaggy, why are you staring so hard at that carton of orange juice?

Because it says, "Concentrate."

Why did the cabbage win the race?
Because it was *a head!*

What's the difference between a guitar and a fish sandwich?
You can't tuna fish sandwich!

Why were the apples thrown off of Noah's Ark?
Only pears were allowed!

Have you heard the joke about the peanut butter?
I better not tell you. You might
spread it!

Which fruit is always teasing the others?

The banana-na-
na-naaaa!

Bit four:

Belly laughs for breakfast

What do mermaids spread on their toast?
Mermalade.

Where do horses eat their morning cereal?
At the breakfast stable!

How does Darth Vader like his toast?
On the dark side!

What's the best way to guarantee breakfast in bed?
Sleep in the kitchen!

What's red, wiggles and flies through the air?
A jellycopter.

What did the computer do for breakfast?
It had a byte to eat.

What did the cup say to the tea bag?
"You're in hot water now!"

Why was the cook so unhappy about working in
the margarine factory?
**She was hoping for something
butter!**

Why didn't the teddy bear eat his lunch?
He was stuffed!

Why do seagulls fly over the sea?
**If they flew over the bay,
they'd be bagels!**

Bit five:
Favourite Scooby Snacks

What do you get when you mix an aardvark
with a pizza?
Ant-chovies!

What's a dog's favourite pizza?
PUParonni!

What do you get when you mix a golfer with
flour, sugar, butter and cocoa powder?
Chocolate putting!

Why do asteroids taste better than chicken sandwiches?
Because they're meteor!

What do little dogs eat at the cinema?
Pupcorn.

What do you get when you mix a cow, a chicken, and a loaf of bread?

A roost beef sandwich!

What do you get when you mix a centipede with a chicken?

Drumsticks for a month!

Bit six:
Least favourite Scooby Snacks

What do you get when you mix a snake with a basket of apples?
A pie-thon!

What did the grape say when the elephant stepped on it?
Nothing. It just gave a little wine.

What amount of salt can hurt?
A pinch.

Where does Scooby buy his food?
At the SUPERmarket!

What do balloons like to drink?
POP!

What does Shaggy serve, but Scooby never eat?
A tennis ball.

What do you call a pretend penne?
An impasta!

I feel like spaghetti tonight.

That's funny, you don't *look* like spaghetti!

Why are frogs always so happy?
They eat whatever bugs them!

Why do watermelons have
fancy weddings?
**Because they
can't elope!**

Bit seven:
Food knock, knocks

Knock, knock!
Who's there?
Figs.
Figs who?
Figs the doorbell. It's broken!

Knock, knock!
Who's there?
Olive.
Olive who?
Olive here. Why are you in my house?!

Knock, knock!
Who's there?
Orange juice.
Orange juice who?
Orange juice coming outside to play?

Knock, knock!
Who's there?
Dishes.
Dishes who?
Dishes me. Who are you?

Knock, knock!
Who's there?
Bean.
Bean who?
Bean a while since I last saw you!

Knock, knock!
Who's there?
Lettuce.
Lettuce who?
Lettuce in. We're cold!

Knock, knock!
Who's there?
Doughnut.
Doughnut who?
**Doughnut ask.
It's a secret.**

Bit eight:
Delicious desserts

Why did Shaggy eat his maths homework?
**Because his teacher said it was a
piece of cake.**

What's white, has a horn and
gives us something nice to eat?
The ice cream van!

Why did the biscuit go to the doctor?
He was feeling a little crumby.

How do you make a milk shake?
Take it to see a scary film!

Why did the baker stop making doughnuts?
She was tired of the hole business.

What does chocolate do when it hears a good joke?
It snickers.

What kind of dessert roams the Arctic tundra?
Chocolate moose!

Why did Scooby go to the doctor after
eating the cupcakes?
Because he got frostingbite.

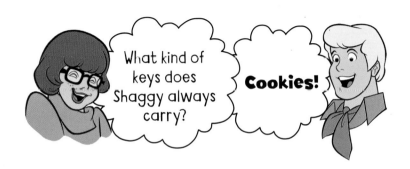

What kind of keys does Shaggy always carry?

Cookies!

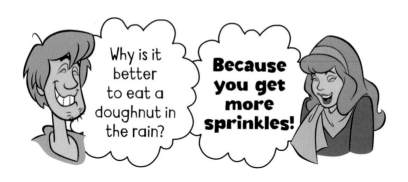

CHILD: How much for a taste of the gingerbread?
WITCH: Don't worry. It's on the house!

How do the Mystery gang make biscuits?
With Scooby-dough!

Why don't they serve chocolate in prisons?
Because if the prisoners eat too much, some of them might break out!

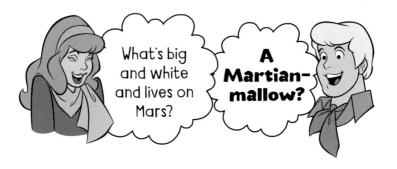

What's big and white and lives on Mars?

A Martian-mallow?

CUSTOMER: Do you have ice cream on the menu today?
WAITER: No, I wiped it off.

Who can serve ice cream faster than a speeding bullet?
Scooperman!

What's a maths teacher's favourite dessert?
Pi.

What grows in the treetops and likes to eat chocolate?
A cocoa-nut.

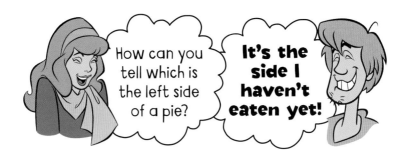

Why did the student work at the bakery?

Because she *kneaded* the dough!

What do you call cheese that is sad?
Blue cheese!

What did the microwave dinner say after it
was packaged?
"Oh no – foiled again!"

What happened to the caveman who saw a sheep
struck by lightning?
He invented the baa-becue!

Why is it difficult to starve on a beach?
**Because of all of the
sand which is there!**

Why did the doctor give mustard to Scooby
when he had a fever?
**Mustard is the best thing for
a hot dog!**

What do you call a pig who's just recovered from a cold?
A cured ham!

What does a pirate like on his salad?
Thousand Island dressing!

How can you tell if a clock is hungry?

It always goes back four seconds.

Why is six afraid of seven?
Because seven eight nine!

Why couldn't the sesame seed stop gambling?
Because she was on a roll!

SCOOBY:
When can we have something to eat?

ASTRONAUT:
At launch time!

Where were the first chickens fried?
In Greece!

What's the world's heaviest soup?
Won-ton soup!

What kind of cup is impossible to drink out of?
A hiccup!

I've heard that polar bears like Mexican food.
Yeah, especially brrr-itos!

What did the police do with the beefburger?
They grilled it!

What do whales eat for lunch?
Peanut blubber sandwiches!

What do you give a poorly lemon?
Lemon aid!

Which is the best day of the week to eat chicken on?

Fryday!

What kind of lunch do you get when a chicken sits on the roof?
Egg rolls!

Which cheese is made backwards?
Edam.

Why did the light bulb get bigger and bigger?
He kept eating watts and watts!

How do seals make pancakes?
With their flippers!

What do you call cheese that
isn't yours?
Nacho cheese!

What do you get if you cross a duck with a cow?
Milk and quackers!

Where did the spaghetti go to dance?
The meat ball!